HOME SERIES

HOME SERIES
BATHROOMS

BETA-PLUS

CONTENTS

P. 4-5
This bathroom was designed by Virginie and Odile Dejaegere.
The old oak floor is from Van Huele.

P. 6
A project by Sophie Campion.
A solid washbasin in Azul Valverde. Taps by Ritmonio.

FOREWORD

The very definition of an intimate and private space, the bathroom is increasingly expected to satisfy new, modern demands. This room has to radiate a sense of comfort, beauty, security. It is a place for relaxation, wellness, escape, whether the design is contemporary, classic or even Baroque in style. More and more attention is devoted to the selection of luxury materials and high-tech gadgets.

This makes the bathroom much more than a purely functional space, turning it into a real living space that deserves a lot of care and attention.

Sometimes this room has all the charm of a living room and the bedroom has to sacrifice some floor space to accommodate the new-style bathroom. Or it can be completely integrated into the bedroom, as an en-suite space for health and relaxation.

These increasingly luxurious and open designs come with higher expectations: design, ergonomics, safety, functionality, aesthetic considerations. All of these parameters need to come together to create a bathroom that is the perfect living space.

The reports in this book feature inspirational examples of bathrooms in a wide range of styles and forms: timeless, ultramodern, rustic, exotic. There are so many different ideas for creative interiors where the bathroom occupies a prominent position.

P. 8
Sphere Interiors created this bathroom.
Fitted units in wengé-tinted oak. Cordoba and Emperador natural stone. Mem taps by Dornbracht.

P. 10-11
Lapidis supplied the exclusive pebbles for the finish in this bathroom, created by Yvette Seder.

EXTREME SIMPLICITY

IN A STREAMLINED BATHROOM

In this report, interior architect Alexis Herbosch from Apluz design consultancy presents one of his renovations: a stylish contemporary bathroom.

The main bedroom/bathroom/dressing room block of this house is harmoniously designed in shades of white and écru, with some dark chestnut notes in the bedroom.

Alexis Herbosch created an opening in the wall to connect the two spaces. Sliding doors separate the rooms and create different atmospheres in this home.

The original bath (Strip by Aquamass) is the eye-catching feature here: its flowing lines continue in the white wall. Pale pine planks were selected for the floor. The washbasins rest on simple blocks, with taps mounted at the front of the unit. The central island between the two washbasins serves as a storage unit.

THE BATHROOM

AS A LIVING SPACE

B rigitte Peten designed this bathroom as a real space for living: painting, carpet, a place to sit. It is comfortable and warm with all the appeal of a living room.

The colours of the painting inspired the designer in her choice of natural stone and wall shades.

P. 16-19
Van Den Weghe supplied and installed the Spanish Ambar stone, with a honed finish.

A NOSTALGIC SPACE

FOR RELAXATION

For years, the English brand Samuel Heath (distributors include Lerou) has steered clear of fleeting trends, producing a top-quality range of authentic taps and bathroom accessories.

These are not trendy retro models that quickly go out of production, but unique products whose value only increases.

This report, featuring the bathrooms of the beautiful Bruges hotel Kasteel De Spycker, presents a large number of Samuel Heath products in sophisticated rooms with a grand siècle atmosphere.

Washbasin taps with crossed handles in polished brass and a standard spout. A bath in an alcove.

A FEEL FOR DESIGN

F or this interior project, Obumex worked with the Van Den Weghe stone company.

The combination of exclusive materials (stone and wood) ensures a timeless, chic and contemporary atmosphere in this bathroom.

The ingenious layout of the space and the large shower deserve particular attention.

Van den Weghe first fired the Ghibli anciento granite to give it a rough look. They then treated the surface with an iron brush to create a velvety, non-slip finish.

A COSY BATHROOM

Jos Reynders Decor renovated this elegant townhouse from 1880 and interior architect Helena van den Driessche designed the interior.

The owners wanted a direct connection between the master bedroom and the bathroom on the mezzanine. The designer used part of the existing dressing room to create a way through to the main bathroom. The bedroom, the bathroom and the dressing room are now one large room. This involved installing a large window and new stairs in the bathroom. The layout, the light, the materials and the absence of tiles combine to produce a very cosy effect.

The high ceilings and windows create a sense of space and ensure that the room is light and airy. Photographs by Lartigue, Cartier-Bresson and Miller.

THE BATHROOM

OF A MODERN PENTHOUSE

S oon after graduating, Magali Van den Weghe was asked to give this 1970s penthouse a young and contemporary look.

She completely restructured the entire space, including the bathroom.

The ultramodern and minimalist atmosphere is the result of the harmony and simplicity of the materials and design: a grey stone for the floors and walls. A streamlined and chic bathroom.

The open shower with two doors in matte glass can be reached from the bathroom and the toilet. Stone by Van den Weghe.

THE HEALING POWER OF WATER

Bart De Beule is an interior architect who waxes lyrical when it comes to bathrooms: we leave the warm waters of the womb to enter the cold world. The cult of water is celebrated in every culture.

De Beule places the curative powers of water at the centre of every bathroom he designs, as a symbol of purity and cleanliness, but also of authentic power, of our quest for security and intimacy.

De Beule's clients are essential to his process of working: their lifestyle and outlook form the basis of the project.

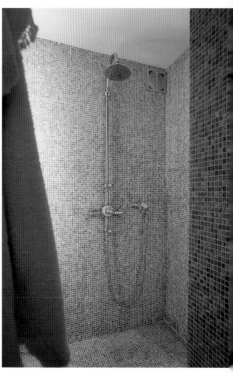

This bathroom was designed for a couple with three children. The interior architect designed a very inviting space in a timeless, natural and restful setting with a number of Provençal accents. The floor is in handmade terracotta tommettes. Bath surround and washbasins in Buxy Ambre stone. Unit by Aldo Bernardi, with cupboards in larch and taps by Volevatch.

In this castle bathroom, the designer opted for reclaimed materials. The old floor in French oak is from Saillart. The bathtub came from a castle and has been restored and integrated into this project. The antique furniture and curios add a very personal touch and create a living-room ambience. The porcelain washbasin dates from the early twentieth century. Taps by Volevatch. The white painted door leads to a spacious shower. The walls are in a latex paint in old English blue.

P. 32-33
This bathroom has a warm, classic atmosphere. The bath and sink are in French Massangis stone, double thickness around the bath. The same Massangis stone on the floor, combined with terracotta cabochons. Taps by Volevatch. The wall above the bath is in mosaic from Saillart.

A SYMBIOSIS

OF BLACK CORIAN AND WOOD

C y Peys Partners created a real zen atmosphere in this bathroom, which they designed as a space for wellness and relaxation. A custom-made bath and shower in black Corian and the same wood that was used for the washbasin surrounds.

The client asked for the showerhead to be integrated into the ceiling. An invisible heating system has been installed around the bath.

The reinforced, black painted wall also contains subtle lighting. The projecting window ensures extra daylight. Art by Cy Peys Partners.

A SCENT OF THE SOUTH

T he Dutch interior architect Bert Quadvlieg has an international reputation for his exuberant interiors, in which durable materials, bright colours and antique-inspired furniture blend together to create a harmonious whole.

In this report, Quadvlieg presents the bathrooms of two beautiful country houses that he created in Théoule-sur-Mer and in Grasse.

The wall behind the bath is in octagonal blue Italian tiles, with yellow enamel. A Heritage bathtub with Lefroy Brooks taps. The floor is in traditional terracotta tommettes.

A colonial atmosphere in this bathroom. The shower is in Balinese stones.

P. 40-41
A view of the central bathtub, in Buxy bleu stone with a shell from Sulawesi above. Perfect symmetry of both washbasins, which are also in Buxy. Taps by Lefroy Brooks. Between the units, a wall of 10x10cm terracotta tiles. All of the woodwork is in Javanese teak; the walls have several layers of whitewash. The terracotta floor is combined with large bluestone tiles.

The floor and part of the wall are in Balinese stone. The vanity unit is in white painted wood, with a mirror above and a wall lamp on one side, both in driftwood.

A charming bathroom in a country house in Grasse. Tiles in white Carrara marble, combined with Verde Vecchio marble. The high panelling has a number of layers of paint, all with old pigments. A Heritage bathtub and Lefroy Brooks taps. An antique mirror in a wooden frame.

P. 44-45
This Provençal bathroom combines Amarello marble with fossil limestone. The panels are painted with a relief finish in two layers of patina. Lefroy Brooks taps.

AN EXCLUSIVE ATMOSPHERE

Costermans, a specialist in the construction of exclusive villas, designed and created the bathrooms in this large, luxury home.

As always, this Antwerp company selected long-lasting and outstanding materials for use throughout the property: exclusive French stone and fittings for this luxurious bathroom with majestic dimensions.

The bathtub is the central feature of the parents' bathroom, with on the left the shower room and the toilet on the right, behind the wall. The stone is from France: a sand-coloured floor in Hauteville marble (honed finish) and a bath surround in polished black Saint-Laurent marble.

FUNCTIONAL AND CONTEMPLATIVE

Isabelle Bijvoet is a young, passionate interior architect. She converted a small children's room with an unused roof space above into an inspiring bathroom that is all about functionality, space, light and cosiness and has a restful, meditative atmosphere.

Every detail in this bathroom reveals Isabelle Bijvoet's passion for functionality in a balanced and elegant setting.

The Turkish hammam was one of the sources of inspiration for this project, as illustrated by the vaulted ceiling, created by Gypel.
A floor of Chinese river stones with white sand joints.
The room is finished in a natural sand-coloured Moroccan tadelakt by ART bvba. Starck basin with Vola taps. Nobi lighting from Fontana Arte. The oak accessories are by Pomd'or (Novia).

EVERY BATHROOM

TELLS A STORY

Ten years ago, Anne De Visscher and her husband Eric Meert started Il était une fois, an exciting, new company designing and creating traditional kitchens and bathrooms.

All of the bathrooms made by this Brussels-based company have a timeless atmosphere and are made to the highest standards of quality. Each bathroom is custom-built to complement the home of the clients, whose wishes form the basis of every design.

The furniture is painted after installation, which allows a great deal of freedom in the use of colours, as can clearly be seen in the projects on these pages.

Left-hand page and above
Il était une fois added a contemporary touch to the classic
timeless look of this elegant home, which dates from around
1900. A space for relaxation in a fin-de-siècle atmosphere.
A Nirvana bath based on an old model rests on a mahogany
base in the centre of a bluestone oval.

Shades of the North Sea: a harmony of colours, from muted
white through to beige, in this panelling, cement tiles and the
marmorino wall plastering.

In this bathroom, Napoleonic-inspired "L'Océan" furniture combines with a "L'Enfant Gâté" shower design, whose chrome pipes and large glass sections give it a modern look. On the floor, bluestone tiles in two different finishes, laid diagonally.
The walls and the furniture are in shades of lilac and mauve, echoed in the window treatments.

A MINIMALIST AESTHETIC

IN BLACK AND WHITE

The team from Cy Peys was commissioned to design this bathroom in a typical loft style and following neutral principles.

Clean architectural lines in black and white, created in long-lasting, distinctive materials.

The black mosaic and the smoked glass contrast with the industrial character of the building. A powerful combination of lines in an ultramodern bathroom: a strong structure and a perfect finish.

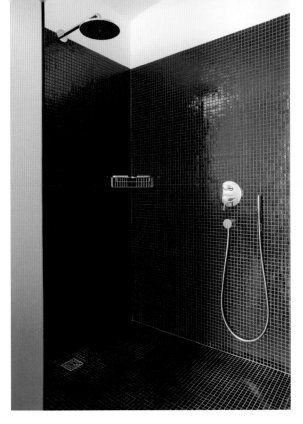

P. 54-57
The parquet floor in the adjoining rooms has been extended into this bathroom to create a sense of space and continuity. Bath and toilet by Duravit and taps by Hansgrohe.

ENGLISH INSPIRATION

The main bathroom/dressing room and the guest bathroom in this exclusive country house were placed in the hands of the Costermans company.

The atmosphere in these rooms is completely in keeping with the rest of the house: classic, elegant and obviously English in inspiration.

A double washbasin unit for her and for him. RVB taps in nickel, 1935 series.

The floor of this English-style bathroom is in a Rosso Verona stone, with Bianco Perlino, sawn to fit.

A shower for two in pale beige mosaic.

A PALETTE OF SOBER SHADES

Over the years, interior architect Bert Desmet has developed a strong reputation as a designer of contemporary and timeless interiors.

This report features a bathroom in one of his projects: an apartment in an exclusive residence. A warm atmosphere for this room, with soft shades and natural materials: wood and natural stone.

Left-hand page and above
Bert Desmet opted here for a sober colour palette and durable materials: beach pebbles from Dominique Desimpel for the floor and the wall above the washbasins, oak shutters and bath surround and a solid, carved washbasin in Anthalia marble. Taps by Dornbracht.

This very spacious shower is clad in pebbles. A Securit glass screen.

A PATINA OF AGE

IN A RESTORED FARMHOUSE

V irginie and Odile Dejaegere (Dejaegere design studio) did the interior design for this restored farmhouse in Wallonia.

They gave the bathrooms of this unique farmhouse an age-old patina through the use of antique wooden floors, a solid marble bathtub and whitewashed walls.

This bathroom, with its marble tub, is a beautiful living space. The old wooden floor is by Van Huele.

Volevatch taps for the washbasin and shower room. The basin, surrounds and shower floor are all in bluestone.

THE MAGIC OF TADELAKT

J an Vanderbeken, founder and driving force behind Odilon Creations, has been a fervent champion of the Moroccan tadelakt technique for many years. Together with his daughter Sigrid, he went to study this technique in the Atlas Mountains with tadelakt master Maalem Moham-med, who revealed his secrets to them.

Tadelakt in its original form has many applications, including Turkish steam baths and hammams. Nowadays it may be used to create walls, floors, bathroom furniture, baths, showers and basins, both inside and out.

This material is as soft as satin and is finished and hardened by hand. The smooth, soft finish of the walls lends an extra dimension to a warm atmosphere. Tadelakt has many advantages: it is both water-resistant and heatproof.

The basic lime plaster is coloured with powder pigments to create vivid shades.

These walls are in tadelakt in a pale "Terre de Sienne" shade.
The section above the washbasin is in grey tadelakt: a perfect match for the old bluestone of the basin. A project by Odilon Creations/Couleurs Tadelakt.

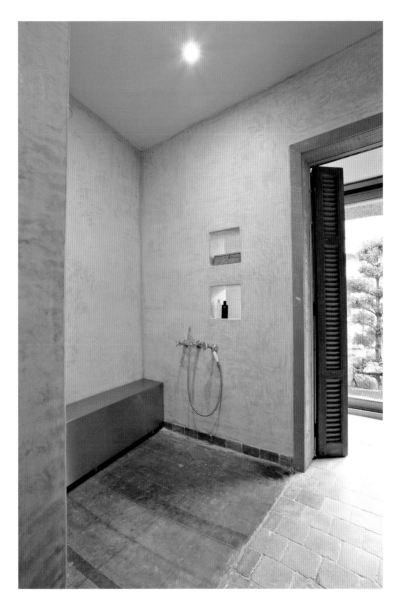

This open shower is in tadelakt: a top-quality, water-resistant finish with a soft feel. A project by Odilon Creations/Couleurs Tadelakt.

This minimalist bathroom is a design by architect Piet De Mey. The floor is in polished concrete. The walls are in grey tadelakt: the nuances change to reflect the natural light.

The cast-concrete washbasin unit was created on site. Odilon Creations applied a grey concrete-look tadelakt finish.

The shower is also in tadelakt. The cement base was covered in a waterproof substance before being given a tadelakt finish, which involves polishing the surface with a river stone and treating it with black soap. The three built-in halogen spotlights create a subdued light.

A harmony of wood and turquoise tadelakt in this bathroom creation by Marie-Sophie Hubert (ETAU architectural studio). The contemporary elements (a washbasin in white porcelain, a bathtub in white acrylic with chrome taps) contrast with the age-old tadelakt technique, created by Odilon Creations/Couleurs Tadelakt. The turquoise tadelakt does not only lend a sense of depth to this space, but also offers superb protection against dampness.

This project by Géraldine Pauwels was created by Odilon Creations/Couleurs Tadelakt. They applied a special layer of cement and a waterproof protective layer to a quick-build construction. The walls and floor of the shower are in anthracite-grey tadelakt. The washbasin unit was cast on site and finished in the same shade of grey tadelakt.

CALM AND COMFORT

A rchitect Stéphane Boens designed this beautiful, English-
inspired country house in the
green outskirts of Antwerp.

Like the rest of the house, the bathrooms
in this unique setting radiate an atmosphere of space, calm and comfort.

P. 72-75
Dominique Desimpel supplied the stone and tiles for these bathrooms. Bath tub on p. 74–75 in solid Carrara marble.

A TRANSFORMATION

WITH A LIMITED BUDGET

n spite of the limited budget for the renovation of this elegant town house, this bathroom project by Cy Peys Partners still features some interesting architectural elements.

The bathroom on the first floor is designed as one large shower room, separated from the dressing room by a glass screen. The floor and walls are in black tiles.

Cy Peys Partners have combined two rooms to create one single space containing a shower room and a dressing room, modernising the look by installing a large window in the wall.
The authentic wooden floor in the children's bathroom has been retained. The shower and bath are combined in this room.

CHARM AND SOPHISTICATION

IN TWO BATHROOMS

The renowned interior specialist Walda Pairon created two bathroom designs that are completely in keeping with her approach to design: a harmonious amalgamation of old and new, with a passion for durable materials, warm shades and exclusive varieties of stone and wood.

A freestanding cast-iron bath tub. Pendragon taps. Blinds in cotton and an antique padded table.

The lamps and the towel rail are designs by Walda Pairon. The eighteenth-century mirror is in ebony.

The shower is in Belgian bluestone.

The beech-wood floor has a painted
finish. Background left, a pine table
with decorative pieces including a
plaster model of a hand.

In this bathroom, Walda Pairon used a very exclusive marble from an exhausted quarry in Brecchia for the floors and surrounds. This has been combined with white Carrara on the walls. The painter used a time-honoured Italian technique to apply the Coristil paints with a knife, creating a wipe-clean finish.

A TASTE FOR RAW MATERIALS

In this industrial loft in Brussels, architect Olivier Dwek, in collaboration with Mathieu Dewitte and Julie Ruquois, created a bathroom that illustrates his affection for raw materials: the walls have a waterproof concrete-coloured cement finish and the floor is in concrete (p. 86–87).

B&H Immobiliën commissioned Olivier Dwek and Gregory Eyndels to restore this Brussels townhouse dating from 1903 (p. 88–89). They sandblasted the original bricks and finished them with an anti-dust varnish. The authentic wooden floor has a dark finish.

Two Starck washbasins rest on the suspended surfaces, in dark tinted wood. Tara taps by Dornbracht. The Nomade Minimal wall lighting is by Modular.

A centrally positioned bath (Bathline Concept Colombe) in sandstone with taps by Ritmonio. Above the washbasin unit, with integrated radiator section and Kusabi basins, a photograph by Thomas Defays (Young Gallery).

TIMELESS CHARM

D ominique Koch is an interior decorator in heart and soul. All of her projects exhibit an inimitable sense of authenticity and traditional craftsmanship, coupled with irresistible charm and passion for detail.

Dominique Koch's company, Zoute Nostalgie, has designed and furnished many different bathrooms in five years.

As Koch works exclusively with coastal properties, her bathrooms are often summery and maritime in inspiration.

In many of her bathroom projects, Dominique Koch shows her fondness for the warm, subdued colours of Scandinavian home design.

The bath is in white Carrara marble. The untreated wooden floor is in elm wood. The art is by Lionel Van Den Bogaert, a gifted painter of the North Sea.

The coat cupboard and guest toilet.
The washbasin is carved from a solid piece of Buxy Clair, a French stone with beautifully understated shades of colour. Painted MDF unit. Taps from Van Marcke.

Shades of aubergine in a washroom in Dominique Koch's house. The rare 18th- and 19th-century wall tiles are from Delft. The terracotta tommettes are also very rare pieces: they date from the early eighteenth century, come from Brittany and have an unusual format (7x7cm). The rounded vanity unit is clad with hand-cut Belgian bluestone. The hand-woven fabric on the left of the picture conceals a radiator.

The washbasin unit is in aged bluestone. The antique mirror was selected by Zoute Nostalgie.

This shower room is connected to the bathroom on the previous page. The
materials are the same: white Carrara marble and an untreated elm floor.

IN SEARCH OF EXCELLENCE

Philippe Van Den Weghe has for years been recognised by renowned architects and interior designers as the top specialist in exclusive natural stone.

He combines a fine nose for the latest trends with real know-how and a passion for his profession.

Without making any compromises, Van Den Weghe aims for the very best quality in stone and in workmanship: his masons and installers are among the best in the field.

This report presents a bathroom project that illustrates Van Den Weghe's reputation for excellence.

P. 94-97

This is the final project by renowned interior architect Jean De Meulder, who died as construction work was beginning. Stavit Mor Interiors and architect Frank Van Laere acted as site managers.
In the steam shower, walls in marble mosaic tiles. The apparently solid benches with built-in atmospheric lighting are in Dolomit Grün.
The large bath in the main bathroom (p. 96–97) is also in Dolomit Grün. The bath functions as a Jacuzzi and as a double shower. A home-technology system allows the owner to fill the bath at the right temperature by telephone.

DISCREET LUXURY

P assionate about decoration and interior design, the three Flamant brothers and their team have for years been creating furniture and other pieces with a timeless look.

With exceptional attention to authenticity, Flamant Home Interiors follow a simple, but brilliant concept: the reproduction of old furniture, which is adapted to suit modern requirements, in a variety of styles, ranging from old England to colonial exoticism and Scandinavian or Provençal style.

Flamant's designs are also very up to date. The world of Flamant is all about discreet luxury and cosy charm with the perfect combination of individuality, comfort and innovation.

All of Flamant's home-design stores devote a lot of attention to the bathroom, so customers can find all sorts of products for bathing: washbasin surrounds in natural or patinated wood and stone, bathroom furniture, mirrors, soap-holders, towels and the Flamant range of bath products.

Flamant bathrooms: a unique mix of old and new. A selection of towels from the Home collection. Baskets from the Havanah series.

A Bocage bath.

An extensive range of bath products.

Two bathroom units by Flamant: in white Calife and in natural oak.

A Dunbar washbasin unit
with a Julia mirror above.

AN INTERPLAY OF PERSPECTIVES

A rchitect Jean-Marc Vynckier's home, whose bathroom is introduced in this report, is in an industrial building and has all the features of the ideal loft: an ocean of space, plenty of light, dramatic proportions and a lived-in, laid-back atmosphere.

Jean-Marc Vynckier's credo is: "Ne rien enlever, ni ajouter" (Remove nothing, add nothing).

It sounds simple, but this desire for authenticity and the quest for the right balance demands a lot of energy and personal investment.

The interplay of perspectives within the property is of prime importance, as this makes it possible to take an entirely new approach to the space.

Vynckier's bathroom is a fine illustration of his philosophy.

Jean-Marc Vynckier lives in a former laundry that has been transformed into a loft.
The floor was cast in black concrete and then polished. The unit is in white Carrara marble with drawers in tropical wengé wood.
Volevatch taps. Halogen wall lighting by Modular.

The standing lamp is a Philippe Starck design.

The shower floor is in white Carrara. Odilon Creations gave the wall a Moroccan tadelakt finish. This method, which is used in hammams, has the advantage of being water-resistant and heatproof.
The bath surround is in oiled wooden planks.

THE WARMTH

OF FRENCH LIMESTONE

L he old, lived-in materials used by Bourgondisch Kruis create a timeless atmosphere in the bathrooms they design. They usually cut the bathroom floor and bath and washbasin surrounds from blocks of hard limestone with a very solid structure. The woodwork (washbasin units, doors etc.) is always in oak.

Bourgondisch Kruis's biggest selling point is the company's long-term project coordination: from the selection, restoration and processing of reclaimed materials to the design of the bathroom by the company's team of interior architects and the installation of the bathroom. The company always respects the client's wishes and can offer a complete service, including details such as the choice of fittings and lighting.

Sawn and honed Burgundy slabs, combined with cabochons in terracotta.

The beauty of Burgundy limestone in the bathroom.

P. 108-109
A complete interior by Bourgondisch Kruis, who supplied all of the natural stone, the old oak doors and wooden floor and the fitted dressing-room units.

Original gothic elements around the mirrors. The taps are by Bourgondisch Kruis and are available in copper and bronze.

TADELAKT BATHROOMS

IN A GUESTHOUSE

T he Valvert guesthouse is the ideal place to stay in the heart of the Luberon.

The aim of the current owners is to emphasise the timeless charm of Provence in an exclusive setting, coupled with a hotel service.

A fountain of ice-cold water for a cooling dip after a visit to the hammam.

The previous owner designed this shower room and bath herself, both finished in tadelakt.

AN EN-SUITE BATHROOM

IN A HISTORIC HOUSE

rchitect Bernard De Clerck redesigned this bathroom in a historic country house.

He retained the existing volumes, and designed an en-suite dressing room/bathroom/shower and toilet, with all of the equipment and storage space concealed in custom-made units, behind oak doors and panels.

De Clerck has created an unusually harmonious whole with a very warm and subdued atmosphere in spite of its large dimensions.

Traditional cabinetmaker Francis Van Damme carried out the construction and installation of the bathroom, using antique elements to make the panels, doors and units in the company workshops, so preserving architectural heritage and managing restoration projects in an authentic way.

P. 114-117

The washbasin unit is in white Carrara marble. Taps by Lefroy Brooks. Lights by Stéphane Davidts.
The wooden floor is old; the units are in new oak. In the centre of the photograph (following pages), an old lantern.

A NEW RUSTIC STYLE

T his bathroom, designed by Doran for Country Cooking, is in solid aged oak.

The LED lighting integrated into the oak panelling provides a starry sky in this cosy bathroom with a unique charm.

The bluestone washbasins are also from the Doran collection.

BATHROOMS FOR LIVING IN

T he success of Flamant Home Interiors owes a lot to the concept of the home-design stores that the group operates in shopping centres throughout Europe and elsewhere in the world.

These exclusive boutiques are furnished like homes, with all the desired accessories: washbasins, mirrors, taps, soap and so on.

In all of these home-design stores, a lot of attention is paid to the bathroom.

These bathrooms are not only intended as a source of inspiration: clients can also have these models installed in their own home. Flamant Home Interiors and Flamant Projects have a large team of staff to make this possible.

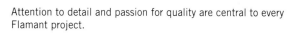

Attention to detail and passion for quality are central to every Flamant project.

A HARMONY OF WOOD

AND PAINTED PANELLING

F or Il était une fois, specialists in the design and creation of home concepts, every interior tells its own story. They therefore give each of their projects an appropriate name.

Here, the "Cottage" project in a country style.

The harmony of woods (oak, afrormosia) and the beige tones of the furniture and panelling create a warm and cosy atmosphere.

HOME SERIES

Volume 4 : BATHROOMS

The reports in this book are selected from the Beta-Plus collection of home-design books: www.betaplus.com
They have been compiled in a special series by Le Figaro in French language: Ma Déco

Copyright © 2009 Beta-Plus Publishing / Le Figaro
Originally published in French language

PUBLISHER
Beta-Plus Publishing
Termuninck 3
B – 7850 Enghien
Belgium
www.betaplus.com
info@betaplus.com

PHOTOGRAPHY
Jo Pauwels

DESIGN
Polydem - Nathalie Binart

TRANSLATIONS
Laura Watkinson

ISBN: 9789089440358

Printed in China

P. 126-127
The beautiful bathroom in Trendson's show home.